CW00516637

2-HOUR STAFF WELLBEING PLAN

- Know your way around stress

- Strategies to minimize & prevent stress in your people

- Get clear on the business case for staff wellbeing support

- Conduct Staff Wellbeing Audit & create your action plan

©2022 Amanda Craven

Amanda Craven MSc(Psychol), Dip Hyp, ADPR, Cert Life Coach
notjustcoaching.com

This book is dedicated to all my clients.

Contents

Introduction

Want to improve staff wellbeing AND positively impact on your organisation's bottom line? Virtually no time or budget to do this? Then you're in the right place because this book will help you integrate your staff wellbeing systems into everyday life, ensure they pay for themselves AND INCREASE YOUR REVENUE!

This guide will help you gain more understanding of stress so that you can better support your teams and make small changes - many with minimal costs - that will have a long-lasting impact on their wellbeing and your organisation as a whole.

The tools provided will enable you to proactively support your teams and in doing so to facilitate the growth of your people and your organisation. In addition they will make it easier for you to present the 'business case' for investing in staff wellbeing to those who hold the pursestrings.

My experience as a manager of multiple teams from early on in my career, and more recently as a mental health professional supporting the wellbeing of staff in other companies, means I fully grasp the importance and impact of preventative measures as well as strategies to combat existing stress. As a manager/team leader you are extremely busy and need information, tools and results fast, so you will not find any fluff in the following chapters - just stuff you need to know in order to make your workplace one where your staff are happy, fulfilled and want to stay.

It will take around two hours to read through the chapters and draw up an outline action plan. You can do it all in one go, or break it down into time chunks that work for you. As you read each section use the table in Chapter 9 to keep notes of what you need to do. The audit template (Chapter 7 - also available as a free downloadable document) will help keep you focused on what needs to be done.

If you want to share any feedback with me, or would like to know about my ability to directly support your organisation's team (limited number of spaces available) please drop me a line at amanda@notjustcoaching.com.

To download (for free!) the HR Staff Wellbeing Audit, the Staff Wellbeing Review, the EFT/Tapping diagram and the Mindfulness scripts that accompany this book please click here:

resources.amandacraven.org/manage-staff-stress-downloads

If you are interested in additional resources that may be helpful, including a video e-course that covers much of the content of this book, please check out:

resources.amandacraven.org/manage-staff-stress

Chapter 1 - Why is it Important to deal with Stress?

Most of us need some pressure, and a little bit of stress, to help us 'perform' in life, both at home and at work. The trouble starts when we lose that sense of balance and stress levels become overwhelming and interfere with our day-to-day functioning. At the time of writing the physical effects of coronavirus are reducing, but the effects of the stress and trauma which have touched everyone in some way are not.

Disruptions to sleep patterns, social contact, physical activity and daily schedules in addition to the uncertainty and trauma which has ensued mean that pre-existing mental health conditions have been amplified and even previously resilient employees have suffered unprecedented stress. According to a report by the World Bank 93% of countries have seen critical mental health services severely disrupted or halted in the wake of the pandemic. If mental health support in organisations was important before 2020, it is absolutely vital now. With health services in crisis it comes down to people like you - a manager, director or team leader - and me, a wellbeing services provider, to do our bit in making the workplace a safe, supportive and nurturing space.

We will look more closely at how chronic stress translates into conditions and behaviours that impact on an employee's quality of life as well as their ability to work effectively later in the book.

For now let's start with a look at the overall economic cost, and main causes, of poor mental health globally to get a sense of the enormity of the problem.

The following figures have been extracted from 'Mental Health & Employers - Refreshing the Case for Investment, Deloitte & Mind Report January 2020':

Economic Cost of Poor Mental Health to Organisations

- £45 billion p.a. (UK)

- $300 billion p.a. (USA)

- $60 billion p.a. (Australia)

Cost Projections

- $16 trillion globally in next 20 years

Primary Causes

- Presenteeism

- Absenteeism

- Leaveism

- Staff Turnover

Presenteeism is the result of employees attending work, or logging in, but not actually able to work effectively (or at all) and is estimated to represent 40% of the above costs.

Absenteeism is of course when a member of staff has called in sick or unable to work for other reasons. (See Chapter 3 for lists of conditions that may not look like they are stress related, but actually are a result of excessive stress.)

Leaveism is a relatively new term which describes both the phenomenon of staff taking annual leave rather than sick leave when they are unable to work and/or the habit of staff taking work home with them or working outside of their paid hours in order to complete their assigned tasks. My experience of working with staff in the third sector highlights this being a huge issue (particularly in health and social care organisations), largely due to the dedication of employees but it is a practice that can be found across all sectors.

Staff turnover costs have already been mentioned, but there are additional costs around recruitment which are more difficult to quantify such as disruption to service and the knock-on effects on teams, departments and the overall efficacy of your organisation.

The above global figures are eye-watering, but let's look at the potential costs of poor mental health to an individual organisation such as yours: it's estimated that stress and other mental health issues cost around **£2000 per employee** per year (Deloitte & Mind Report 2020). So if your business employs 40 people this means you could be 'losing' **£80 000 per annum**. A sum that would undoubtedly make a great impact on your bottom line and in some cases the sustainability of your organisation.

Let's go under the bonnet and explore what stress actually is - you may be surprised!

Chapter 2 - Define and Understand Stress

> Are 'stress', 'anxiety' and 'worry' the same thing?

The terms are often used interchangeably but there are in fact some key differences between them. Here is how the American Psychological Association describes them:

STRESS = typically caused by external triggers eg work deadline (short-term) or chronic illness, financial worries (long-term)

ANXIETY = persistent, excessive worries that don't go away, even in the absence of a stressor

WORRY = the state of being anxious and troubled over actual or potential problems

As stress is the area of mental health that you as a people manager can most easily influence, we are primarily concerned with stress here. However, as some of the causes and symptoms of each can be very similar, much of what we cover will apply to **all** these states. It's important to remember that each of the above is a normal state that is triggered by short-term life challenges. Problems arise when the challenge is prolonged and/ or when we have (or feel we have) no control over the cause of stress.

Stressors come in all shapes and sizes and may be longstanding or new. In cases of complex childhood trauma experienced by people working for you, the stressor may no longer exist but if appropriate help and support were not given at the time your employee may well still be on 'high alert' and easily triggered. This can mean that they may react in an unexpected way to a question or a comment that was not intended to be 'loaded'.

If you want to know more about the 'legacy' of childhood stressors there are some excellent publications on Adverse Childhood Experiences (ACE's) and you'll find some referenced at the end of the book.

Examples of 'Stressors' (the first few are more commonly associated with childhood experiences, though not exclusively):

- Neglect
- Poverty
- Bullying
- Complex childhood trauma
- Trauma
- Violence in the home
- Unsafe home
- Bereavement
- Abuse (physical, emotional, sexual, psychological)
- Relationship issues
- Family member with mental health issues
- Caring responsibilities
- Financial difficulties
- Work deadlines and pressures
- Issues with colleagues
- Poor physical health (self or family member)

- Mental or psychiatric conditions that are undiagnosed or untreated

We humans have amazing coping capacities but they are designed to work in the short term and for short periods of time. A stressor or perceived danger will trigger defence responses from our body and mind. The responses that our brain and body will attempt are:

- Flight
- Fight
- Freeze

These responses actually date back hundreds of thousands of years when threats to cave-dwellers' survival were essentially *physical* (attack from animals or other tribes, climatic or environmental) and *immediate*. The first call our brain would make was to **flee** the danger (we had the most chances of surviving intact if we could escape). Failing that we would assess our strength and resources and prepare to **fight** the 'attacker', leaving a **freeze** response to be a last resort. Unfortunately, the 'old' part of our brain that controls our innate responses hasn't caught up with the fact that most 'threats' in our modern world are not situations that we can run from or fight and often does not serve us well.

In some cases the flight or fight bodily responses (sweating, increased heart rate and respiration, adrenaline rush, need to evacuate bladder or bowels, to name but a few) will occur whether we are facing an interview panel or a violent intruder. When a person is overwhelmed by the perceived danger they are facing, and fleeing or fighting the perpetuator is not an option, a state of freezing or fainting is triggered as a last resort. Going back to our cave-dweller illustration, dropping to the ground with a low pulse rate and shallow breathing gave us a chance of survival as we may have gone unnoticed or appeared already dead.

Whilst the body is in a state of threat response controlled by that very old part of our brain, the 'newer' thinking brain goes off-line - which is why we can't think straight or express ourselves very eloquently at times of stress.

The adrenaline and other neuro-chemicals produced in the processes are supposed to enable us to get out of danger and then recede once the threat is over. As you can see though, most of the stressors in the list can potentially go on for years rather than a few minutes or - tops - a few hours. In the case of prolonged stress this means that our body is flooded with 'chemicals' it cannot cope with and they become toxic, potentially leading to the conditions we'll be looking at in the next chapter.

I find this a fascinating topic which I go into in more detail in my workshops, but this book is about giving you the essentials so I'll leave it there for now. Let's move on to looking at how you can recognise signs of stress.

Chapter 3 - Recognise Stress

You might think you can easily recognise a stressed employee and there are indeed some very obvious symptoms. But take a look through the following lists of symptoms and you may be surprised at the many different ways that stress can present.

Behavioural Symptoms of Stress

If you think back to the brain's responses to stress which result in it effectively going 'offline' it makes sense that an employee who is under stress has difficulty carrying out day-to-day functions. The following list is not exhaustive but gives you a good idea of what to look out for:

- poor concentration

- low energy & mood

- forgetfulness

- irritability

- insomnia

- inability to relax or switch off

- difficulties in communication

- inability to keep still

Psychosomatic Symptoms of Stress

I think it's really important to clarify the meaning of 'psychosomatic' here as it can sometimes be interpreted as 'imaginary' and therefore not real. 'Psyche' indicates the origin of the symptom is in the mind and 'somatic' tells us the symptom is manifested in the body ('soma' is the Greek word for body). Messages from the brain can create genuine physical changes in the body. As a very simple example, try imagining a fresh juicy, bright yellow lemon. Smell the zesty, invigorating fragrance. As you cut into it think about the juice dripping from your knife. Will you be putting a slice in a cool, refreshing drink, or using it to give flavour to a meal or a cake? Is your mouth salivating yet? If it is, you've just created physical changes in your body with your thoughts!

So, to resume, the symptoms and pains caused by stress are absolutely real and debilitating, and include:

+ palpitations

+ headaches

+ sore throat

+ gastro-intestinal problems including IBS (Irritable Bowel Syndrome)

+ back or neck pain

+ dizziness

- sweating

- muscle tension

- panic attacks*

*There is a bonus chapter on panic attacks with practical tips that you can apply or share with staff so they are able to support someone experiencing a panic (or anxiety) attack.

Quiz
Which of the following diseases & conditions have been linked to stress?
A. Psoriasis/Eczema
B. Rheumatoid arthritis
C. IBS (Irritable Bowel Syndrome)
D. Alzheimer's Disease
E. MS (Multiple Sclerosis)

Would you be surprised to know that research has linked all of the above to stress? Here is a more complete list which will no doubt grow as more studies reveal new evidence.

Diseases linked to Stress

- Cardiovascular disease

- Parkinson's disease

- Alzheimer's Disease

- Diabetes

- Strokes

- Auto-immune diseases eg MS (Multiple Sclerosis)

- Inflammatory diseases

- Certain types of cancer eg breast cancer

If you want to read more about the effects of stress on the body check out the excellent books 'When The Body Says No' by Dr Gabor Maté and 'The Body Keeps the Score' by Bessel Van Der Kolk. Links to both are located in the Reading List at the end of the book.

Other Conditions that may result from Stress

- Addictions

- OCD (Obsessive Compulsive Disorder)

- Phobias

- C-PTSD (Complex Post Traumatic Stress Disorder) or PTSD (Post Traumatic Stress Disorder)

As we've seen, the consequences of prolonged stress are pretty much unlimited. Many anxiety disorders - social anxiety, performance anxiety, generalised anxiety disorder, to name but a few - are borne out of unrecognised or unaddressed chronic stress. Staff who feel overwhelmed may seek their own ways of 'coping', by numbing, masking, and distracting themselves from the symptoms.

An employee might want to numb their unwanted feelings simply in an attempt to feel 'normal' and this can result in drinking more and more alcohol, relying heavily on prescription drugs, smoking cannabis or taking other substances to self-soothe. This is how addictions can develop.

Feeling overwhelmed and not being able to control the source of the stress can lead to a need to take control of other areas in order to compensate. Obsessive Compulsive Disorder (OCD) may result and you might observe someone being very controlling of certain tasks or spaces at work, or implementing very inflexible procedures. Other behaviours such as hoarding and being unable to let go of objects may also develop from a need to keep control and self-soothe.

Phobias can develop from a past negative experience or may be linked to previous panic attacks and may need to be addressed if they interfere with someone's wellbeing or ability to function at work.

If a member of staff experienced ongoing difficulties in childhood (sometimes in later life), or has been involved in a serious accident or incident at any time they may experience 'triggers' and be hyper sensitive to certain work situations or pressures that appear uneventful to others. Examples could be if an employee is challenged about a decision, asked to lead a meeting or travel to an unfamiliar location for work. Complex Post Traumatic Stress Disorder (C-PTSD) or Post Traumatic Stress Disorder (PTSD) could have developed and the person will need to receive specialist help. Complex PTSD indicates that there is more than one traumatic experience and/or the exposure to the traumas was prolonged (in the case of extended childhood abuse, for example).

In any instance where behaviour is impacting on their ability to work effectively or on their quality of life suggesting your employee contact their doctor would be a good first port of call. If there are also physiological symptoms present a doctor will be able to arrange exploratory tests, and a diagnosis will help clarify the best treatment route.

Emotional/psychological support will always benefit an employee, provided they are open to this. There is still a lot of stigma attached to such support so it is important to make it as 'mainstream' as possible in your organisation, whilst ensuring individual referrals are always discussed in confidence. One organisation I work with used to provide staff access to a counsellor but found take-up was very low. When I began running 'Drop-In Wellbeing Coaching' sessions they were booked out from the start! I imagine that the scope of the counselling and my coaching was pretty similar but there were a few crucial differences:

- Everyone, from the CEO down was clearly briefed on what the sessions were for (offloading onto a neutral professional, trouble-shooting problems at home or at work, support for mild-moderate mental health issues eg anxiety or low mood)
- Everyone was invited to book (in confidence) and given access to this support
- Managers were encouraged to proactively identify staff who may be struggling with an issue and conversations about the support became 'normalised'
- Staff knew these sessions were available every month and a schedule of dates was drawn up a year at a time
- The use of the term 'wellbeing coaching' felt quite ordinary and reduced any stigma of accessing support

There are many types of effective psychological and complementary therapies available to help your people deal with stress as well as to help prevent it reaching critical levels and promote general wellbeing. We will look at the different options in Chapter 8 and I will show you ways to find accredited therapists.

The next chapter looks at the connection between boundaries in your workplace and staff stress.

Chapter 4 - Boundaries and Wellbeing

Boundaries are essential in all parts of our life. Boundaries mean clarity. Clarity in work boundaries reduces stress in the workplace and improves productivity.

Imagine the following scenario in your workplace:

It's just after 9.05 am on Monday and your team has gathered in the conference room for the 9.00 scheduled weekly briefing. Most people have been at work since 8.30 and you sense their impatience to start the meeting although a couple of employees haven't arrived yet. You chat informally one-to-one with a few people whilst the rest of the group catch up on personal news from the weekend. Out of the corner of your eye you notice Barbara leaning over Tom, knocking his notepad to the floor, to whisper something to Ryan. The noise levels rise but you don't want to start until everyone's here.

You go back to your seat and start scribbling a list of things you want to discuss and mentally check off who isn't in the room yet. The usual suspects - Carole and Chris. They achieve some great results but do everything their own way. You don't want to say anything in case they quit but you know others are starting to complain that they get away with too much and expect their colleagues to cover for them. At 9.16 Carole and Chris swing through the door, laughing loudly and continue their conversation as they squeeze in between a couple of people at the end of the table. Chris turns to talk to Maria and places his hand on her back as he speaks. She looks really uncomfortable and looks over towards you. You wish you could say something but you don't know how you could without creating an atmosphere.

At 9.20 you get everyone's attention and stand at the white board. You ask for suggestions of what they'd like to discuss today and write up the list. It takes ten minutes to complete, at which point Melissa stands up, hugging her notepad with a list of questions she had for the team. She looks red-faced. "I have a video meeting now and have to go. This meeting should have been over by 9.30am."

As she leaves the room Carole bursts out laughing and jokes about 'Merlissa's OCD' making her impossible to work with. "She's probably autistic as well!", she quips. "Did anyone see that documentary last night on autism and Tourette's syndrome, by the way? Hilarious!" A few people snigger and the room breaks up into chats about TV shows.

You throw your hands in the air and say lamely "Okay guys. Let's call it a day. Have a good week, do your best and see you next Monday. Try to be on time everyone!"

Okay, so this **may** seem exaggerated but I have personally witnessed each and every 'boundary transgression' or absence of boundaries in my own working life, and I'm sure many will resonate with you, too.

Just imagine the impact of such a 'boundary-less' working environment for the individuals employed there. Think about the stress of not knowing what is deemed acceptable, what is expected of you, and the general lack of guidance. Think about the impact of the ensuing chaos on staff morale and the productivity of such a workplace.

Let's break down boundaries into categories so you can easily work out which, if any, need reviewing in your business. I have divided this list into what I call 'Macro Boundaries' (which are more structural and visible in many cases) and 'Micro Boundaries' (which are more about interpersonal interactions).

Look through the lists and ask yourself if all these points are crystal clear to your staff, and how they are communicated (eg in contracts, in mission statements or in information packs for new staff). As with all the lists in this book, they are not exhaustive and aim to prompt a general consideration of appropriate boundaries in your organisation.

MACRO BOUNDARIES

TIME

- Working hours/days

- Start and finish times

- Core working time

- Proportion of working time devoted to different tasks

- Lateness policies

- Frequency and duration of meetings

- Expectations for out of hours tasks

- Leave policies & expectations (vacations, sickness absence)

COMMUNICATION

- Internal communication protocols (what platforms used, for what purpose)

- External communication protocols (what platforms used, for what purpose)

* Sharing of work/personal contact details

* Meeting agendas (who is responsible, when/how are they communicated)

* Meeting minutes and action plans (who is responsible, when/how are they communicated)

* Clear targets and goals

PHYSICAL

* Proximity

* Appropriate touch and gestures

* Designated work space(s)

* Shared or communal areas

* Parking areas

MATERIAL

* Equipment assigned to an individual (terms & conditions)

* Equipment considered as 'shared' (how, when etc)

* Dress/uniform codes

* Client or customer gifts – what is okay to give/receive

MICRO BOUNDARIES

Note: It is more difficult to create specific rules for many of these areas but some can easily be incorporated into your 'Mental Wellbeing Statement' (see Bonus Chapter 4)

EMOTIONAL

    •Sharing personal stuff

BELIEFS

    •Openness

    •Acceptance

    •Spiritual/religious

    •Inclusivity

MENTAL

    •Different 'filters' and perceptions

    •Different perspectives

    •Different ways of processing information/instructions

In addition to the above, you may want to be aware of the need for individual employees to be clear on individual boundaries around their time, energy and personal resources. The next chapter will look at ways you can broach any concerns or sensitive topics.

Chapter 5 - Difficult Conversations

Although this chapter is entitled 'difficult' conversations, your interactions with staff around their mental health and wellbeing do not have to be difficult and awkward.

As we saw at the end of the previous chapter, if you already have an open culture regarding discussions on mental wellbeing it should be quite natural to check in with employees about whom you have concerns.

The following conversation starters can take place just as easily at the water cooler as in a review meeting, as long as you are out of earshot of other employees:

"I've noticed that…"

"I'm wondering if everything's okay…?"

"Do you fancy going out for a coffee/having a walk-and-talk?"

"I thought you looked a little [down/worried] in the meeting this morning…"

"Your [colleagues/line manager] mentioned that…Is there anything I can do to help?"

Or, for times when your team member has told you about difficulties they're experiencing:

"How can I support you right now?"

"What can we as an organisation do to help you?"

They key is avoiding tones and words that could be construed as accusatory. Keep your questions open, gentle, and compassionate.

If the person you're talking to is very low and refers in any way to 'just ending it all' or says something along the lines of 'everyone would be better off without me' then you must get more direct. Instead of asking 'you're not going to do anything silly, are you?' You must take the bull by the horns and ask outright, "Do you have plans to end your life?". Or, "Are you really thinking of killing yourself?".

If you believe that your employee is suicidal you must take immediate action and follow whatever protocols are in place in your organisation or in your state/country to make an urgent referral to the appropriate agency/medical body. Keep the person with you until you have arranged the necessary help, and always err on the side of caution.

If someone is very low but not specifically suicidal make sure you give them the number for a 24/7 helpline in your country (eg look up samaritans.org or samaritansusa.org).

If you feel you can improve the way staff are supported or create more openness around mental health issues take a look through the ideas in the next chapter and in the HR Mental Wellbeing Audit template.

The following Wellbeing Review & Toolkit can easily be integrated into staff reviews/appraisals or supervision sessions to ensure you can check in regularly with your team. You are welcome to copy it as it is, or to use it as a template and source of ideas. The Review & Toolkit are free to download for purchasers of this book - go to resources.amandacraven.org/manage-staff-stress-downloads .

....

STAFF MENTAL WELLBEING REVIEW & TOOLKIT

EMPLOYEE NAME:

DATE:

Hello!

This review is for you to complete alone before you meet with [your manager] for a mental wellbeing review. This review will take place [alongside a supervision session/during an informal chat] [once a year/once every 6 months...] and will help us to support your mental health at work. This document is a working document, to keep an open dialogue and use points raised to review how we as your employer can best support you.

The first section will be kept on file by [manager] and the second section is for you to keep and use as a self-help tool.

The information on this form is confidential and will [not be shared/be shared with HR with your permission].

1. When do you feel, and work, at your best in your job? (eg 'After a relaxing weekend off.' 'When I have clear instructions & deadlines.')

[ ]

2. What things at work make you feel stressed or anxious? (eg 'A noisy office.' 'Someone raising their voice.')

[ ]

3. How do you feel and how do you react when you're stressed or anxious? (eg 'I feel hot.' 'I forget things.' 'I'm snappy.')

[ ]

4. What helps reduce these stress or anxiety symptoms? (eg 'Get some fresh air.')

5. Do you have any pre-warning signs of stress symptoms?

6. What could you/we do at the first sign of the symptoms?

7. What can **we** as your employer do to make your job less stressful?

8. What can **you** do to make these things less stressful?

9. Is there anything you would like to share with your managers about your preferred working style or your wellbeing at work? (e.g. preference for written or verbal deadlines, time management support)

Employee Name:

Signature: Date:

Manager Name:

Signature: Date:

....

WELLBEING TOOLKIT

(for staff to complete and keep for themselves)

1. *Make a list of things that have made you feel calmer or improved your mental wellbeing in the past, or things you believe may be helpful.*

Include a variety of ideas that take different lengths of time to use at home and at work.

Examples include:

- Listen to relaxing music

- Go for a walk

- Phone a friend

* For more ideas, please see below

Ideas for your toolkit:

◆   Read or listen to a self-help book

◆   Have a favourite meal

◆   Jogging

◆   Have a bath

◆   Watch something funny

- Make a list of 10 things I'm grateful for

- Treat myself to a small gift (from a magazine to a new gadget or item of clothing)

- Sing

- Have a massage

- Write down how I'm feeling

- Call a helpline

- Book in with a coach or therapist

- Join a self-help forum or Facebook group

- Change the layout of your desk/office/bedroom

- Have an early night

- Do some physical exercise

- List all my achievements

- Do yoga or meditation

- Wash your hair/shave and put on some clothes that make you feel good

- Light a fragrant candle

◆ Do a jigsaw

2. Create a Self-Care Package for Yourself

Make a list of around 10 items you can put in a bag or a box for yourself to dip into on days you're feeling down or are struggling with something (see below for suggestions):

1.

2.

3.

4.

5.

6.

7.

8.

9.

10.

IDEAS FOR SELF-CARE PACK

compilation of feel-good music

funny book

fluffy socks

sachet luxury hot chocolate

scented candle

bubble bath

photos of good times

face masks

book of short stories

collection of inspirational quotes

voucher to spend online

magazine

DVD or list of films

essential oil

puzzle book

colouring book and colour pens

scrap book or mood board for pictures of dreams & plans

Chapter 6 - Effective Stress-Management Strategies

Stress-management needs to be built into the organisational culture so it is pro-active and not just reactive.

By using regular wellbeing check-ins you will have a good handle on what the workplace stressors are so your first port of call should be looking at the feasibility of

- eliminating or reducing the identified culprits.
- creating support systems

As an organisation you can promote certain behaviours and strategies on an ongoing basis:

- Physical relaxation

- Mindfulness or meditation

- Better sleep routines

- Physical activity

- Time in nature

- Create balance between work/family/'me time'

- Use of self-help therapies and books (see Bonus Chapters & Suggested Reading List)

- Professional help (see Chapter 8 for ideas)

Following the coronavirus pandemic there has been a greater focus on mental health in all workplaces but very recent research has highlighted some huge differences between what employers believe they are providing and how much staff feel supported. According to studies published on employeebenefits.co.uk in August 2021, 39% of employers questioned stated they actively support staff mental health, yet only 16% of employees actually felt supported.

Where possible, leading by example is crucial. Obviously there are exceptional times when you as a manager are required to work late or deal with issues out of hours, but these periods should be the exception, not the rule. If your team sees you leaving on time, valuing your leisure time and do not generally receive messages or calls from you out of hours then you are creating a healthy blueprint for your organisation's culture and values. You are an ambassador and role model for your company - both for the clients/customers you serve and your staff. If you find that you are not able to model the healthy balanced approach you wish for your employees it may be time to arrange a review of your own stressors and look at ways you can adjust your workload.

The following ideas for improving staff wellbeing are also found in the list of wellbeing initiatives in the HR Wellbeing Audit (see next chapter). As you will see, there are many that cost nothing to implement - you just need to invest some time to get them in place. Check out Chapter 8 for details of more therapies and a guide to finding professional, accredited therapists.

If you'd like to create an in-house self-help library for your staff there are some suggested books listed in the Appendix that would be a great place to start.

Wellbeing initiatives to consider:

Promote/subsidise gym memberships
Encourage staff to move for 5 minutes every hour
In-house meditation classes
Open communication about mental health
In-house Wellbeing Manual & Toolkit
Buddy system (Junior with Senior staff)
Arrange 'Walk & Talk' meetings* (outdoors/green space if possible)
No work 'out of hours' policy
Professional mental health support ('Drop-In' or on request)
Time off for exercise
On-site clothed massage sessions (eg Indian Head Massage)
Healthy office snacks & drinks
Mindfulness Practice (see Bonus Chapter 2)
Staff Mental Wellbeing Plan for every employee
Flexible working hours
Smoking cessation campaign
Green plants

Indoor & Outdoor games & activities
Yoga classes
Nominating a 'Health Ambassador'
Team or individual competitions (eg 'step' challenges)
Vouchers for holistic treatments
Quiet Space

* Research by Living Streets (livingstreets.org.uk) - a UK-based charity that promotes everyday walking - has produced some startling figures about the effects of incorporating walking into organisational culture: When employees take part in regular exercise it typically results in a performance increase of about 15%!

Let's now take a look at how to gather and collate information about your wellbeing initiatives in a useful document - your Staff Wellbeing Audit.

Chapter 7 - Your Wellbeing Audit & The Business Case for Staff Wellbeing

*"This workshop confirmed that staff wellbeing actions are **business** decisions, not fluffy 'extras' if there's money left at the end of the year."*

Operations Manager who attended the workshop that this book is based on.

Let's start by reminding ourselves of the costs of poor mental health at work:

- 17.5 million working days per annum lost due to poor mental health (UK)

- £45 billion estimated costs to businesses

- Costs due to : Presenteeism (40% of costs), Absenteeism, Leaveism, Staff Turnover

- Average costs of £2000 per employee per annum

- Return on investment of effective mental wellbeing interventions = c. 5%*

(Taken from Mental Health & Employers – Refreshing the Case for Investment, Deloitte & Mind Report January 2020)

* Quoted as being as much as 15% in other studies

We've already touched on the costs to your organisation of poor mental health (back in Chapter 1) and the aim of *this* chapter is to help you quantify those costs and pull together a clear action plan.

Research has shown how employees who feel they are cared for by their organisation will do their best for you as a manager or team leader, will stay with you for longer and will be an amazing ambassador for your company (employeebenefits.co.uk/38-wellbeing-support-improves-productivity/.

The recent pandemic has meant that most of your teams have, at some point, been forced to work from home. The staff I have worked with have either loved this - or hated it. I haven't come across many who didn't mind either way. As we come out of this crisis, it's crucial that you listen to your staff and provide choice and flexibility *where possible*. For some of your people, working from home has made it easier to juggle their roles, for others it has cut them off from human contact and/or led to feelings of being trapped in a caring role from which they have no respite.

Listening to your employees and creating opportunities for ongoing dialogues will guide you through the best choices to make to ensure ongoing wellbeing **and** productivity.

The following audit template will help you to collate all the relevant information you need to cost your staff wellbeing initiatives and to present an accountable plan to your Director/

Board. As with the previous Wellbeing Review you are welcome to use it in its entirety or lift the sections that are relevant to your organisation. You can download your copy for free from resources.amandacraven.org/manage-staff-stress-downloads .

not just coaching

coaching – therapy – training

HR Staff Wellbeing Audit

Company Name:

Completed By:

Date:

Reminder – Benefits of a Staff Wellbeing Plan

Happier,
healthier staff

Cost of
Sickness Absence

Staff Retention

Need to Recruit Temps

Performance

Costs of Presenteeism

Productivity

Costs of Leaveism

Profit

Ease of
Recruiting New Staff

Costs of Poor Mental Health & Return on Investment of Wellbeing Actions

In order to be able to evaluate the effectiveness of interventions you provide in your organisation, it's important to have measures in place. Recalculate your costs in 12 months to compare and see what impact your actions have had.

Costs of Poor Mental Health

Annual cost of sickness absence in your department/business?	
Average cost of sickness absence per employee per year?	

Proportion/cost of absences due to poor mental health *

(e.g. stress, anxiety, depression) It is believed that 40-50% of total sickness absence is due to poor mental health, so you could use a percentage to calculate your costs here:

For the department/business as a whole:	
Average cost per employee per year (divide total cost by number of staff):	

*Remember that there are many physical illnesses caused by stress (see List A), and staff may prefer to cite physical rather than psychological or emotional symptoms.

Returns on Investment (ROI)

The interventions in Table 1 have been identified through research as having a direct positive impact on the mental wellbeing of staff.

Tick the ones you provide or would like to provide & write the estimated annual cost of each one in the final columns. There is plenty of space for adding your own ideas on pages 5-6.
Write the totals here:

Overall cost to organisation	
Cost per employee	
Multiply figures by 5% * * **for predicted return on investment (money saved and additional earnings through increased productivity) or add actual figures**	

** Return on investment of effective interventions for mental wellbeing is between 3 – 15%.
It is generally believed that 5% is an average ROI.

Table 1 - Wellbeing Interventions

Actions	Have	Would Like	Total Est. Cost £/$	Est. Cost PP £/$
Gym membership				
Moving for 5 minutes every hour				
Meditation Classes				
Open communication about mental health				
In-house Wellbeing Manual & Toolkit				
Buddy system (Junior with Senior staff)				
'Walk & Talk' meetings (outdoors/green space if possible)				
No work 'out of hours' policy				
Professional mental health support ('Drop-In' or on request)				
Time off for exercise				
On-site massage sessions (eg Indian Head Massage)				
Healthy office snacks & drinks				
Mindfulness Practice				
'Staff Mental Wellbeing Plan' for every employee				

Table 1 - Wellbeing Interventions

Actions	Have	Would Like	Total Est. Cost £/$	Est. Cost PP £/$
Flexible working hours				
Smoking cessation campaign				
Green plants				
Indoor & Outdoor games & activities				
Yoga classes				
Nominating a 'Health Ambassador'				
Team or individual competitions (eg 'step' challenges)				
Vouchers for holistic treatments				
Quiet Space				

Table 1 - Wellbeing Interventions

Actions	Have	Would Like	Total Est. Cost £/$	Est. Cost PP £/$
Total costs/Costs per employee				

List A – Physiological Symptoms, Conditions & Diseases that have been related to Stress in Research

Headaches & migraines
Sore throat
Gastro-intestinal problems including Irritable Bowel Syndrome (IBS)
Back pain
Neck/shoulder pain
Dizziness
Excessive sweating
Muscle tension
Panic attacks
Psoriasis/eczema & other skin 'flare-ups'
Rheumatoid arthritis
Inflammatory conditions
Multiple Sclerosis (MS)
Alzheimer's Disease

57

Now let's take a more detailed look at the different therapies available to address stress and related conditions. I'll also give you some pointers about how to find certified, insured professional therapists.

Chapter 8 - Therapies for Reducing and Preventing Stress

Please note that the following information is for guidance only and is correct at the time of writing. The lists of therapies are not exhaustive and are designed to show the breadth of wellbeing approaches out there, and to inspire you to look for different ways of supporting your people.

'Talking' Therapies to consider

- Counselling
- Hypnotherapy
- Life Coaching
- Psychotherapy

'Physical' Therapies to consider

- Alexander technique
- Aromatherapy
- Bowen technique
- Massage therapy
- Reflexology
- Shiatsu

Other Therapies

- Art therapy

- Dance therapy
- Healing
- Mindfulness-Based Stress Reduction
- Nutritional therapy
- Reiki
- Yoga Therapy

The following information about each discipline is an outline only and has been sourced from the organisations in point 4 if not otherwise stated:

<u>'Talking' Therapies (may be delivered in person, by phone or via video link)</u>

- **Counselling & Psychotherapy**
  Counsellors and psychotherapists are trained professionals who usually work with clients over a period of time to address issues including loss, stress and anxiety (see <u>bacp.co.uk</u> for more details).

- **Hypnotherapy**
  Hypnotherapy is a skilled communication aimed at directing a person's imagination in a way that helps elicit changes in some perceptions, sensations, feelings, thoughts and behaviours. It is often used to promote relaxation, reduce stress, improve sleep patterns and facilitate new habits and behaviours. (More information from <u>hypnotherapy-directory.org.uk</u>).

- **Life Coaching**
  Life coaches use diverse strategies to support clients through periods of change or stress. It's possible to have group coaching

sessions as well as one-to-one. (More details from _lifecoach-directory.org.uk_)

'Physical' Therapies to consider

- **Alexander technique**

The Alexander Technique works through assisting a person to improve the perception of their posture and movement. It may help people find relief from unnecessary tension and its effects. This can help to bring about a positive sense of well-being.

- **Aromatherapy**

Aromatherapy is the therapeutic use of essential oils to help deal with everyday stresses and emotional well-being.

The oils may be applied in combination with massage or the aromatherapist may suggest other methods.

- **Bowen technique**

Bowen therapy is a soft tissue remedial therapy that involves the therapist using fingers or thumbs to move over muscle, ligament, tendon and fascia in various parts of the body. This therapy can be effective to help relieve everyday stresses and revitalise the whole person.

- **Massage therapy**

Massage may be found to bring relief from everyday aches, reduce stress, increase relaxation, address feelings of anxiety and tension, and aid general wellness. There are a variety of techniques practised including fully clothed options.

- **Reflexology**

Reflexology is based on the belief that there are reflex areas in the feet and hands which are believed to correspond to all organs and parts of the body. Some practitioners may also include work on points found in the face and ears. It may alleviate and improve symptoms such as everyday stress and tension.

- **Shiatsu**

Shiatsu is a touch based therapy that applies pressure to areas of the surface of the body through loose comfortable clothing for the purpose of promoting and maintaining wellbeing.

Shiatsu is a Japanese word that literally means finger pressure and derives its theoretical and practical roots from the ancient traditions of Oriental medicine.

Other Therapies

- **Art therapy**

Art therapy is a form of psychotherapy that uses art media as its primary mode of expression and communication. (Information from British Association of Art Therapy - baat.org)

- **Dance/Movement Therapy**

Dance therapists can work with people to help them improve self-esteem and reduce stress and anxiety. Dance/movement therapy is a versatile form of therapy founded on the idea that motion and emotion are interconnected.

- **Healing**

The history of Healing stretches back for thousands of years. Nowadays most Healers view their work as a natural and purposeful energy based process which, from mostly anecdotal evidence, is believed to help relieve everyday stress and provide a sense of physical and emotional revitalisation.

The client remains fully clothed and may be seated or lying down.

- **Mindfulness-Based Stress Reduction**

Mindfulness Based Stress Reduction (MBSR) therapy is a meditation therapy, though originally designed for stress management, it is also used for treating conditions including depression, anxiety, chronic pain and immune disorders.

- **Nutritional therapy**

Nutritional therapy promotes good health, performance and personal care though the application of scientific nutrition. A nutritional therapy practitioner may help clients to improve their sense of health and well-being.

Nutritional therapy may improve health, support those with chronic conditions and encourage a sense of well-being.

- **Reiki**

"Reiki" (ray-key) is Japanese for 'universal life energy', a term used to describe a natural system to help bring about an improved sense of wellbeing and deep relaxation.

The recipient remains clothed and comfortably lies on a couch or sits on a chair. The practitioner gently places their hands non-intrusively, on or near the body using their intuition and training as a guide. There is no massage or manipulation. Reiki can be used on the person as a whole, or on specific parts of the body. It is also possible to receive Reiki at a distance.

- **Yoga Therapy**

Those who wish to develop their natural wellbeing may find yoga therapy a useful route. Yoga therapy is taught by yoga teachers with additional training and experience in the therapeutic adaptation and application of yoga. People may be taught one-to-one or in a therapy group setting.

Through practising a yoga therapy programme the participant may, for example, become more aware of posture and breathing. She/he may also find regular practice can help to promote relaxation, aid sleep and relieve tension; it may help to contribute to an increased sense of wellbeing and a positive mood.

It is your responsibility to conduct your own research and verify that your chosen practitioner(s) is/are accredited to work in whatever country or state you may be. Here are some tips to get you started:

1. Use your network contacts to ask for recommendations
2. Search 'accredited [hypnotherapists]' in your area
3. Search 'professional body for [hypnotherapists]' and follow links for members who seem appropriate
4. In the UK check out the Complementary and Natural Healthcare Council (cnhc.org.uk), The General Regulatory Council for Complementary Therapies (grcct.org) or the Federation of Holistic Therapists (fht.org.uk).
5. In other countries search for 'licensed [therapists]'

6. Always research therapists on your shortlist - check qualifications, insurance status, reliable reviews - and make sure they are recognised in your country/state
7. Contact therapists you like the sound of and arrange a meeting/call
8. Ask about trial sessions or a break clause in a contract in case the therapy doesn't work well in your business
9. Be clear about arrangements and contracts
10. Make sure you receive required documentation (eg insurance certificate) before work begins

Chapter 9 - My Action Plan

Use this table to log the actions you need to take to create your Staff Wellbeing Plan:

WHAT	WHEN	DONE

WHAT	WHEN	DONE

Bonus Chapter 1 - Panic Attacks

The Diagnostic and Statistical Manual of Mental Disorders ('DSM-5', the go-to mental health reference book for medical practitioners) describes a panic attack as 'an abrupt surge of intense fear or intense discomfort that reaches a peak within minutes, and during which time 4 (or more) of the following symptoms occur:

- Palpitations, a pounding heart, or accelerative heart rate

- Sweating

- Trembling or shaking

- Sensations of shortness of breath or smothering

- Feelings of choking

- Chest pain or discomfort

- Nausea or abdominal distress

- Feeling dizzy, unsteady, light headed, or faint

- Chills or heat sensations

- Numbness or tingling sensations

- Feelings of unreality or detachment

- Fear of losing control or "going crazy"

* Fear of dying'

Panic Disorder may be diagnosed when panic attacks recur unexpectedly and avoidant or maladaptive behaviour ensues.

If the attacks are prolonged (eg more than 30 minutes) or frequent it's essential to get checked out by a doctor to eliminate physiological causes.

What to do if someone has a panic attack:

1. Help them get comfortable. Remind them that this will pass. If it's appropriate and if they are OK with being touched , you can stroke their hand or arm.

2. Talk calmly - about anything, and reassure - using a soothing, even monotonous voice. Reassure them that you will stay with them until it passes.

3. Gently distract them by drawing their attention to something you can both see, and slowly and calmly talk about it. You could use a soothing calming voice to tell them a story or anecdote but don't ask them questions or try to make them laugh at this point.

4. When you can see that their symptoms are reducing and the person is becoming calmer, offer a drink of water if available and ask if they would like to rest somewhere, if feasible, or go home.

Advice to give an employee who suffers from panic attacks:

1. When you feel the early signs of a panic starting calmly take yourself to a quiet space, well-ventilated if possible. If you're driving pull over at the earliest safe opportunity to do so.

2. Sit, or lie down, and drop your shoulders. Let your body become as floppy and heavy as you can, and remind yourself that this will pass.

3. Focus your gaze on anything you can see – your feet, a picture, the sky, a blotch on the ceiling and keep your breathing as soft and gentle as possible. Don't try to breathe deeply – your body will enable you to get as much air as you need. You can breathe in and out through your nose, or in through your nose and out through your mouth. Whatever feels more comfortable for you.

4. You may notice your symptoms coming like waves, so just imagine riding those waves, going with the flow, not trying to stop anything from happening.

5. You will find that your symptoms begin to subside, so remain comfortable and still and allow the feelings of calm to reach every part of your body.

6. When you've felt calm for a few minutes, allow yourself to gently move and sip water if available.

7. Take your time before getting on with your day, and rest – if you can, and need to.

8. Your panic attack is over, and you coped brilliantly! So feel proud of yourself, and
remember that you can deal with any future attacks just fine. Be proud of how you
managed!

Remember that if the attack lasts longer than 30 minutes, or recurs frequently, you should go to your doctor to rule out any physiological causes of the symptoms.

If the attacks continue and you have had a medical check up, you may benefit from having a course of hypnotherapy with a registered clinical hypnotherapist to work through the underlying causes and triggers.

HELP SOMEONE HAVING A PANIC ATTACK: KEY POINTS

- Talk slowly and gently
- Take them somewhere quiet and calm
- Let them sit or lie down & invite them to let their body go heavy and floppy
- Suggest they close their eyes or gently focus their gaze on something
- Ask them to breathe gently but don't over-focus on breath
- Continue to talk in slow, monotonous tones
- Remind them this will pass
- Tell them a story, describe an object you can both see, or read a mindfulness script

---

- Offer sips of water if available
- Once their symptoms have subsided, let them rest until they are able to have a gentle walk around

Bonus Chapter 2 - Mindful Meditation Scripts

You, or someone else in your organisation, may read out the following scripts to staff as part of your in-house stress-management provision. Alternatively you may wish to play the scripts directly from the audio book.

The meditations here are deliberately very short - lasting around a minute each. This keeps them highly manageable and research has shown that even this length of 'time out' is a great way of calming anxiety.

Mindful Meditation 1: Focus on an Object (Calming)

Make yourself comfortable, let your shoulders go down...gently breathe in and out through your nose, or in through your nose and out through your mouth. Just focus your attention on an object you can comfortably see from where you are...

Really look at what you can see...notice everything about it...the colour or colours...shadows or shading...what about the texture...? What shape is it? Are there several shapes within it...? Is there light reflecting off any part of this object?

Notice how your body becomes more relaxed, the more you focus on your object.

Enjoy this moment of stillness for a few moments longer. When you're ready...stretch out your arms...take a comfortable, relaxing breath...and smile!

Mindful Meditation 2 : Focus on Your Feet (Calming)

Make yourself comfortable, let your shoulders go down...gently breathe in and out through your nose, or in through your nose and out through your mouth. Now just think about your feet for a moment...with or without looking at them...

just notice what they are in contact with...are they completely on the ground or bed...or is it just your heel...or the ball of your foot that's touching a surface?

Let your eyes close if they're not already closed.
Can you feel the fabric of your socks or tights on your skin?...How does it feel?...Maybe you have shoes or slippers on...can you feel where they are touching your feet?

Wriggle your toes...and notice all the parts of your feet that move when you do this. Focus on your right foot...can you feel any tiny, micro movements?...What about its temperature? Does it feel warm...or cool...? Light...or heavy?...

What about your left foot...? Does it feel exactly the same as the right one?...What differences can you notice...?

Let the muscles in your feet become loose and floppy...just allowing any tension or tightness to melt away...when they feel as relaxed as you can ever imagine them feeling...let that softness gently flow up your body...spreading a feeling of wellbeing and calm, gently, slowly...right up to the top of your head. Then release it...all the way back down to your feet...a gentle wave of calm...

When it reaches your feet again you can become aware of your surroundings and slowly re-open your eyes.

Mindful Meditation 3: A Tree (Energising)

Make sure your feet are touching the floor, and close your eyes.

Imagine what it's like to be a tree...your branches stretching outwards and upwards towards the sky...your roots reaching far down into the earth...weaving their way through the layers and layers of soil...connecting with the very essence of energy from the earth.

Feels those roots stretching as far as they can...notice what it feels like to absorb that energy through every cell and fibre of your roots. Maybe the energy looks like lines of light...imagine what colours it could have as it rises up from the earth, refreshing and energising your whole body from the tips of your toes to the top of your head.

When every part of you feels invigorated by this energy and light...stretch...smile...and open your eyes!

Bonus Chapter 3 – Tapping or Emotional Freedom Techniques (EFT)

You can share this information with your teams or you could appoint someone in your organisation who is comfortable with it to lead an in-house Tapping session.

Tapping is a technique that combines verbal and non-verbal ways of connecting with the mind-body and releasing tension. The nine points that you tap on are energy or meridian points, similar to the acupoints used in Chinese medicine (eg acupressure & acupuncture):

1. Karate Chop point - little finger side of your hand (either hand)

2. Crown of your head

3. In between your eyebrows

4. Outer side of your eye

5. Below eye socket

6. Under your nose/above top lip

7. Below bottom lip

8. Collar bone (one or both)

9. Edge of armpit

10. Back to karate chop point

You need to tap on each point with the tips of 2-3 fingers from one hand as you're saying your 'mantra' (see below for suggestions). You can get a free-of-charge download with a diagram by going to <u>resources.amandacraven.org/manage-staff-stress-downloads</u> and a demonstration of tapping from my 'not just coaching' YouTube Channel linked below. :

<u>not just coaching YouTube Channel</u>

The beauty of this technique is that it's quick, easy and totally portable (many of my clients tell me they often use it in the car before going into an appointment or a meeting). It's possible to tap for anything from a couple of minutes upwards, and the words (although more effective if said out loud) may be said in your head. I've been using it for years and find it a very simple way to ground myself in times of stress.

You can use these ideas for what to say, but it really is best to use your own words that describe what you're feeling. Make sure that you create a sense of balance between the symptoms you are experiencing and your acceptance that this is how it is at this moment. You understand it will pass, and are not fighting it.

Suggested 'Mantras':

(Said whilst continuously tapping each point in turn with two or three fingers)

"Even though I have this feeling of [describe feeling/sensation in as much detail as possible] I completely accept this."

OR

"Even though I'm feeling [describe feelings/sensations], I accept this."

See Appendix for more resources on EFT/Tapping. There's also a free diagram you can download from resources.amandacraven.org .

This short introduction probably doesn't do the technique justice so I highly recommend watching the videos to get a better understanding of what it is, and what it can do.

Bonus Chapter 4 - Your Mental Wellbeing Statement

Creating a Mental Wellbeing Statement for your department/ division or the organisation as a whole is a great way of communication a vital part of your organisational culture ie your attitude to mental health. As with all types of corporate statements it must reflect what *actually* happens and not what you'd *like* to happen.

In addition to the notes in the 'Micro Boundaries' section in Chapter X, consider what you would say about the following in your statement:

•Importance of mental health

•Open-door policy

•It's okay not to feel okay

•Summary of support

•First port of call

Here's a sample statement you could use to get you started:

We at [organisation/department] greatly value the mental wellbeing of our staff.

The measures we have in place include [list of resources or initiatives].

You can access and use our Staff Wellbeing Toolkit [located in...] at any time, and you are welcome to let [your line manager] know if you are struggling with anything, whether home- or work-related.

We believe that it's okay not to be okay and will do what we can to help you.

Please remember that as a member of our team you are never alone.

Signed [name/position]

Your Notes

APPENDIX – REFERENCES AND SUGGESTED READING LIST

Please note that some links are from my Amazon Affiliate List and I may earn a small commission if you purchase after clicking on the links.

A full copy of the list is available from the usual place resources.amandacraven.org/manage-staff-stress-downloads

Deloitte/Mind Wellbeing at Work report

deloitte.com/content/dam/Deloitte/uk/Documents/consultancy/deloitte-uk- mental-health-and-employers.pdf

Mind guide for Managers

mind.org.uk/media-a/5761/mind-guide-for-line-managers-wellness-action- plans_final.pdf

The Self-Care Revolution (Suzy Reading)

A practical book that is written with compassion and full of tips to remind us to take care of ourselves:

https://amzn.to/2Jxz8b8

When the Body Says No (Gabor Maté)

A fascinating read about the impact of stress and personality types on our physical health:

https://amzn.to/3lvdXUr

The Body Keeps the Score (Bessel Van Der Kolk)

Mind, Brain and Body in the Transformation of Trauma:

https://amzn.to/3Dd0NWg

Books by Peter Levine:

Peter has worked extensively with clients who have suffered many forms of trauma and has shared ground-breaking understanding of how the body reacts to trauma – and how it can heal. Two great reads:

Waking the Tiger

https://amzn.to/2I1bO5h

In an Unspoken Voice

https://amzn.to/3mxewOX

Rewire your Anxious Brain (Pittman & Karle)

Great explanations of fear, anxiety and worry and practical tips to reduce them.

https://amzn.to/37nbXIO

Introducing Emotional Freedom Techniques (EFT) (Judy Byrne)

A pocket-sized, easy to read introduction to using tapping techniques:

https://amzn.to/36uUDT3

The Little ACT Workbook (Sinclair & Beadman)

A pocket-sized, easy to read book full of practical tips to help manage stress, depression and anxiety.

https://amzn.to/3g19nMl

The Tapping Solution: A Revolutionary System for Stress-Free Living (Nick Ortner)

https://amzn.to/3mqbte1

The Little Pocket Book of Mindfulness (Anna Black)

Some simple ideas for making life more mindful.

https://amzn.to/2KRjw2K

The ACEs Revolution!: The Impact of Adverse Childhood Experiences (John Trayser)

https://amzn.to/3gsBPZ7

The Adverse Childhood Experiences Recovery Workbook (Schiraldi, Penning et al)

Heal the Hidden Wounds from Childhood Affecting Your Adult Mental and Physical Health

https://amzn.to/3zbcf2h

Adverse Childhood Experiences ACEs: why all the fuss (Ed Wendy Thorley)

England, the North East and Cumbria

https://amzn.to/3sEeYyy

About the Author

Amanda is a Clinical Hypnotherapist, Life Coach, Psychologist and Author based in North Yorkshire in the UK with a global client base.

She has been coaching managers and staff in the non-profit, public and private sectors for over 7 years and supports organisations' teams through drop-in coaching sessions, workshops and 1-1 manager coaching.

In order to be able to reach out to more stressed-out managers and employees she has written this book and created a series of digital courses and materials to accompany it.

Thank you!

Thank you so much for buying this book!

I hope you find it useful and I always welcome feedback and/or ideas for future books and workshops that would help you.

Remember that you can download all the accompanying materials for free here
resources.amandacraven.org/manage-staff-stress-downloads

If you want to get in touch with me directly you can email me at amanda@notjustcoaching.com.

Go create a stress-free workplace for you and your team!
Until next time!

Amanda

Printed in Great Britain
by Amazon

36764252R00051